MOTIVATING
QUOTES
FOR
MOTIVATED
PEOPLE

P9-DDS-262

0 43422 69554 6

Copyright © 1998 Great Quotations, Inc.

All rights reserved. Written permission must be secured
from the publisher to use or reproduce any part of this book,
except for brief quotations in critical reviews or articles.

Cover Design by Roy Honegger

Published by Great Quotations Publishing Co.,
Glendale Heights, IL

Library of Congress Catalog Card Number: 95-81339

ISBN 1-56245-241-X

Printed in Hong Kong

FOREWARD

Today's business world is often viewed as a frantic scramble to the top, with little time for reflection. This collection of motivational quotes gives you many thoughts worth thinking as you strive to reach your goals. To motivate people, you've got to engage their minds and their hearts. This compilation of common sense and genius will motivate you at work, increase your effectiveness in writing and communication and above all impress your boss and clients with your business acumen.

Enjoy!

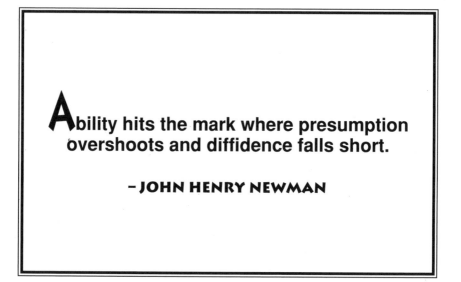

Ability hits the mark where presumption overshoots and diffidence falls short.

– JOHN HENRY NEWMAN

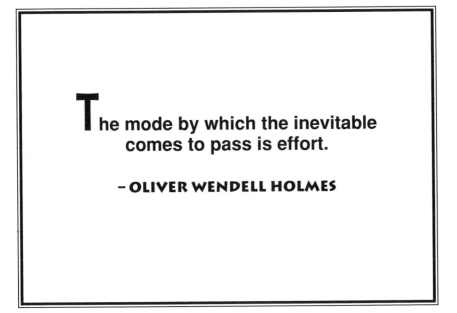

The mode by which the inevitable
comes to pass is effort.

– OLIVER WENDELL HOLMES

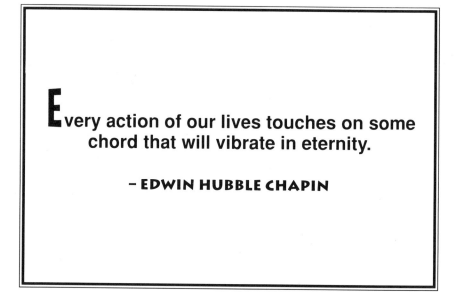

Every action of our lives touches on some chord that will vibrate in eternity.

– EDWIN HUBBLE CHAPIN

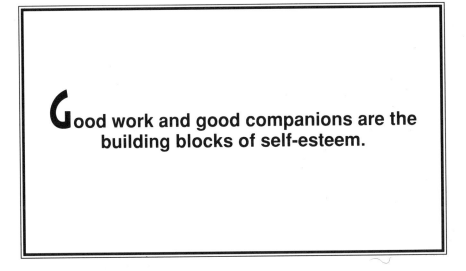

Good work and good companions are the building blocks of self-esteem.

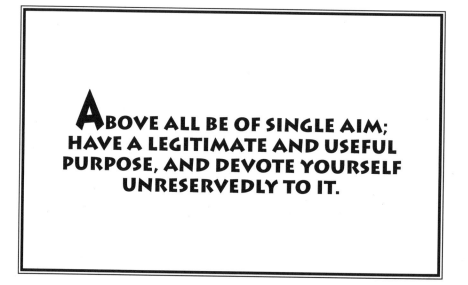

ABOVE ALL BE OF SINGLE AIM;
HAVE A LEGITIMATE AND USEFUL
PURPOSE, AND DEVOTE YOURSELF
UNRESERVEDLY TO IT.

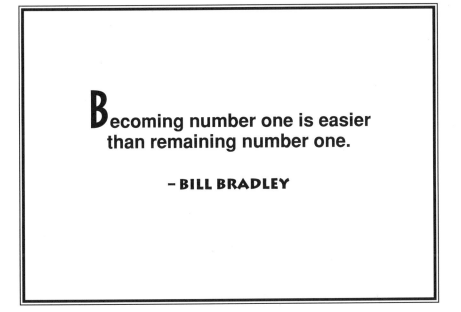

Becoming number one is easier than remaining number one.

– BILL BRADLEY

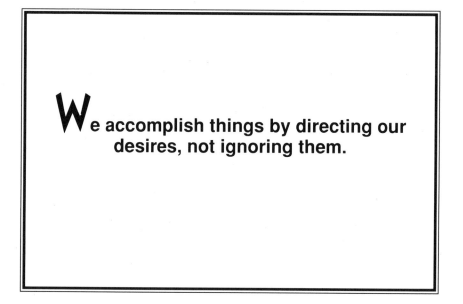

We accomplish things by directing our
desires, not ignoring them.

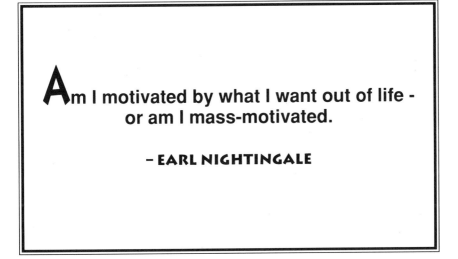

Am I motivated by what I want out of life -
or am I mass-motivated.

– EARL NIGHTINGALE

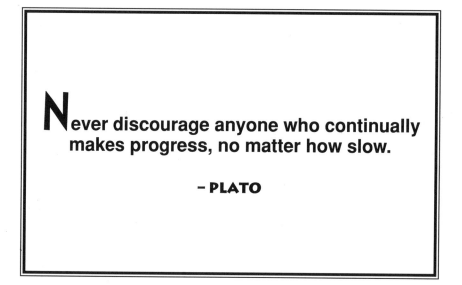

Never discourage anyone who continually makes progress, no matter how slow.

– PLATO

Tell me and I'll forget; show me and I may remember; involve me and I'll understand.

– CHINESE PROVERB

He who makes great demands on
himself is naturally inclined to make
great demands on others.

– ANDRE GIDE

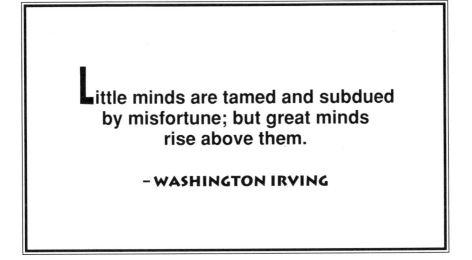

Little minds are tamed and subdued
by misfortune; but great minds
rise above them.

— WASHINGTON IRVING

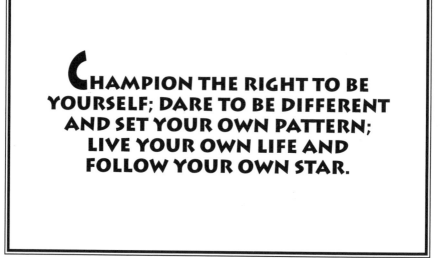

CHAMPION THE RIGHT TO BE
YOURSELF; DARE TO BE DIFFERENT
AND SET YOUR OWN PATTERN;
LIVE YOUR OWN LIFE AND
FOLLOW YOUR OWN STAR.

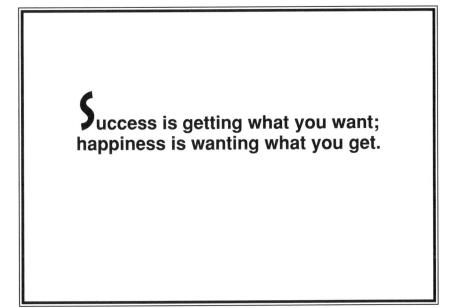

Success is getting what you want;
happiness is wanting what you get.

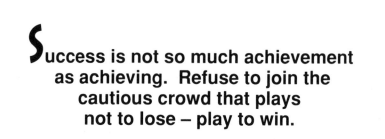

Success is not so much achievement
as achieving. Refuse to join the
cautious crowd that plays
not to lose – play to win.

– DAVID J. MAHONEY

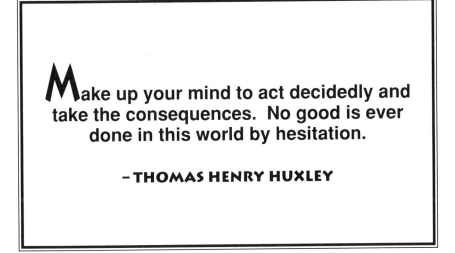

Make up your mind to act decidedly and take the consequences. No good is ever done in this world by hesitation.

– THOMAS HENRY HUXLEY

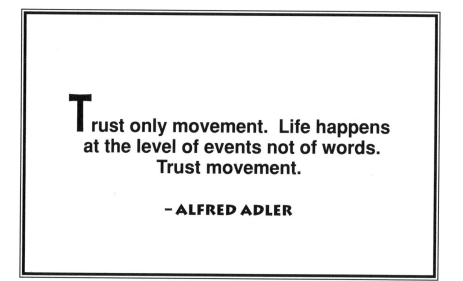

Trust only movement. Life happens
at the level of events not of words.
Trust movement.

– ALFRED ADLER

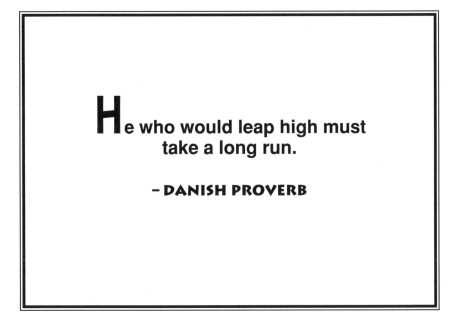

He who would leap high must take a long run.

- DANISH PROVERB

If you aspire to the highest place,
it is no disgrace to stop at the second,
or even the third, place.

– CICERO

If your daily life seems poor, do not blame it, blame yourself, tell yourself that you are not poet enough to call forth its riches.

– RAINER MARIA RILKE

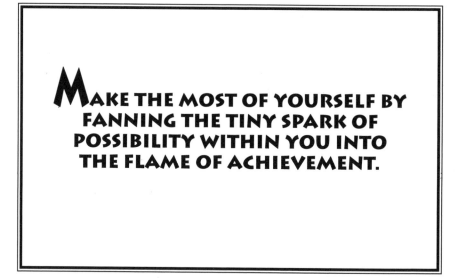

MAKE THE MOST OF YOURSELF BY
FANNING THE TINY SPARK OF
POSSIBILITY WITHIN YOU INTO
THE FLAME OF ACHIEVEMENT.

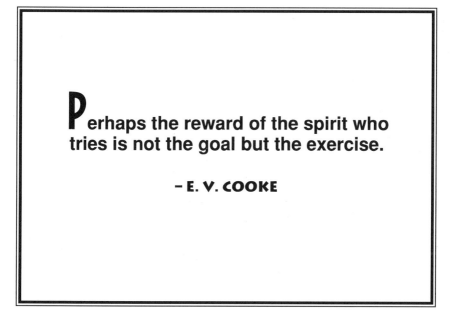

Perhaps the reward of the spirit who tries is not the goal but the exercise.

– E. V. COOKE

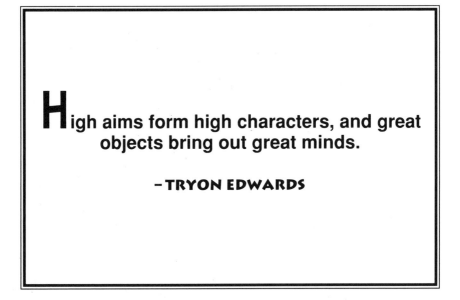

High aims form high characters, and great objects bring out great minds.

– TRYON EDWARDS

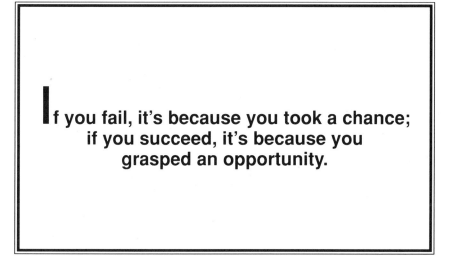

If you fail, it's because you took a chance; if you succeed, it's because you grasped an opportunity.

We must always change, renew, rejuvenate ourselves; otherwise we harden.

– GOETHE

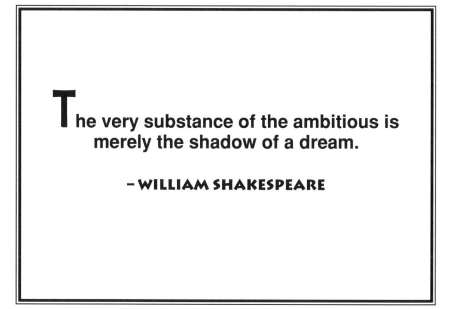

The very substance of the ambitious is merely the shadow of a dream.

– WILLIAM SHAKESPEARE

Everyone is a genius at least once a year. The real geniuses simply have their ideas closer together.

– GEORGE C. LICHTENBERG

Don't let life discourage you; everyone who got where he is had to begin where he was.

- RICHARD L. EVANS

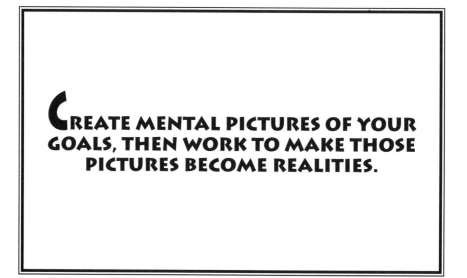

CREATE MENTAL PICTURES OF YOUR GOALS, THEN WORK TO MAKE THOSE PICTURES BECOME REALITIES.

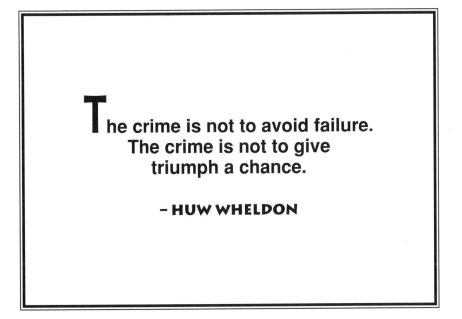

The crime is not to avoid failure.
The crime is not to give
triumph a chance.

– HUW WHELDON

The most important thing in life is to see to it that you are never beaten.

– ANDRE MALRAUX

If you wish success in life, make perseverance your bosom friend, experience your wise counselor, caution your elder brother and hope your guardian genius.

– JOSEPH ADDISON

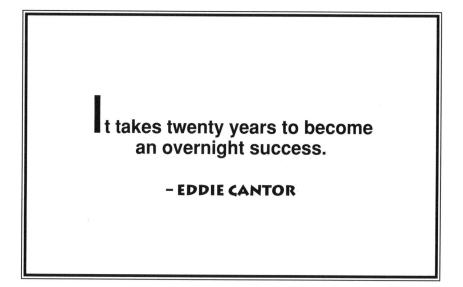

It takes twenty years to become
an overnight success.

– EDDIE CANTOR

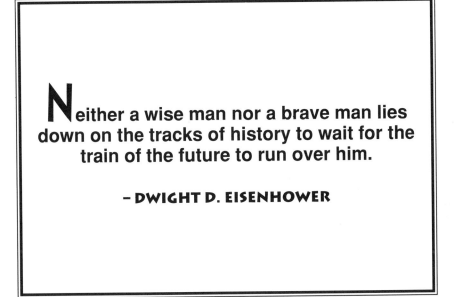

Neither a wise man nor a brave man lies down on the tracks of history to wait for the train of the future to run over him.

– DWIGHT D. EISENHOWER

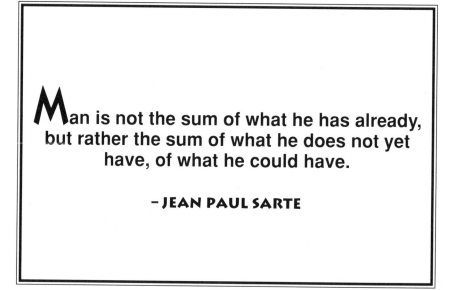

Man is not the sum of what he has already,
but rather the sum of what he does not yet
have, of what he could have.

– JEAN PAUL SARTE

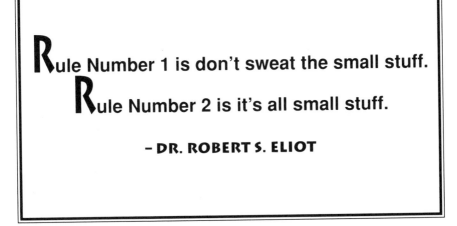

Rule Number 1 is don't sweat the small stuff.

Rule Number 2 is it's all small stuff.

– DR. ROBERT S. ELIOT

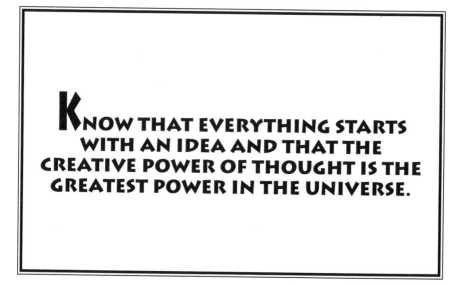

KNOW THAT EVERYTHING STARTS WITH AN IDEA AND THAT THE CREATIVE POWER OF THOUGHT IS THE GREATEST POWER IN THE UNIVERSE.

A life spent making mistakes is not only more honorable but more useful than a life spent doing nothing.

– GEORGE BERNARD SHAW

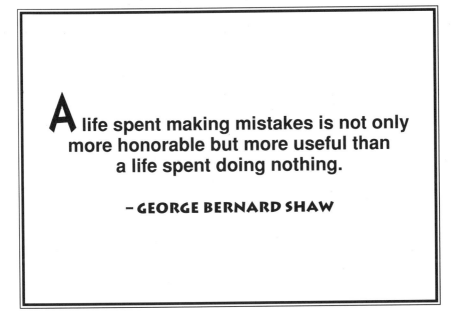

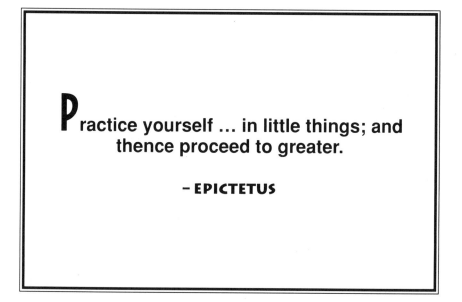

Practice yourself ... in little things; and
thence proceed to greater.

- EPICTETUS

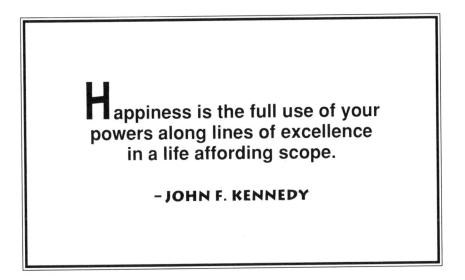

Happiness is the full use of your
powers along lines of excellence
in a life affording scope.

– JOHN F. KENNEDY

Fame is what others give you. Success is what you give yourself.

If one advances confidently in the direction of his dreams, and endeavors to live the life which he has imagined, he will meet with a success unexpected in common hours.

– HENRY DAVID THOREAU

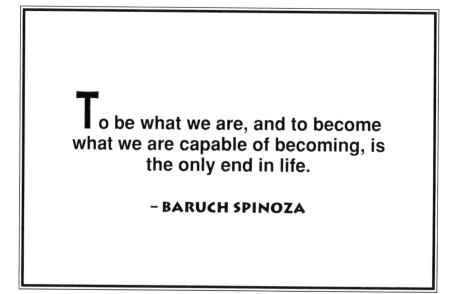

To be what we are, and to become
what we are capable of becoming, is
the only end in life.

– BARUCH SPINOZA

Let no one be like another, yet
everyone like the highest.
How is this done?
Be each one perfect in himself.

– JOHANN WOLFGANG VON GOETHE

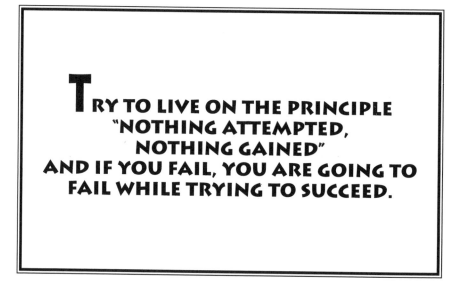

TRY TO LIVE ON THE PRINCIPLE
"NOTHING ATTEMPTED,
NOTHING GAINED"
AND IF YOU FAIL, YOU ARE GOING TO
FAIL WHILE TRYING TO SUCCEED.

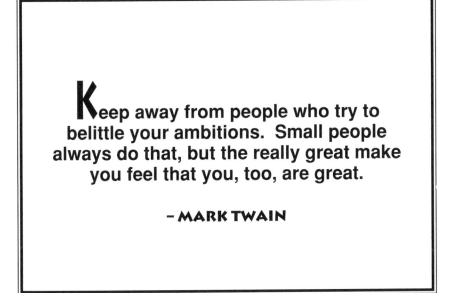

Keep away from people who try to belittle your ambitions. Small people always do that, but the really great make you feel that you, too, are great.

– MARK TWAIN

Press on. Nothing can take the place of persistence. Talent will not; nothing is more common than unsuccessful men with talent. Genius will not; the world is full of educated derelicts. Perseverance and determination alone are omnipotent.

– CALVIN COOLIDGE

I've been absolutely terrified every moment of my life and I've never let it keep me from doing a single thing that I wanted to do.

– GEORGIA O'KEEFE

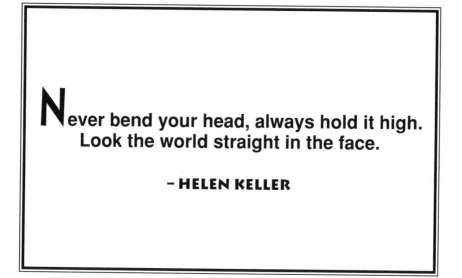

Never bend your head, always hold it high.
Look the world straight in the face.

– HELEN KELLER

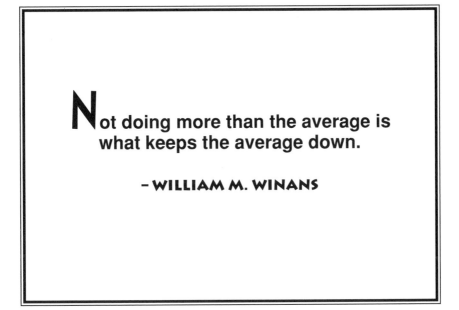

Not doing more than the average is what keeps the average down.

– WILLIAM M. WINANS

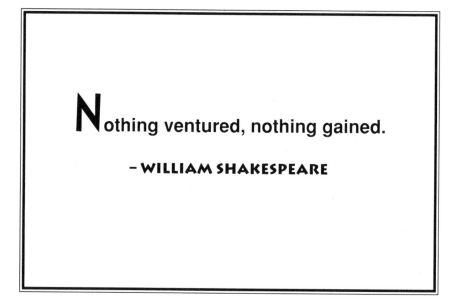

Nothing ventured, nothing gained.

– WILLIAM SHAKESPEARE

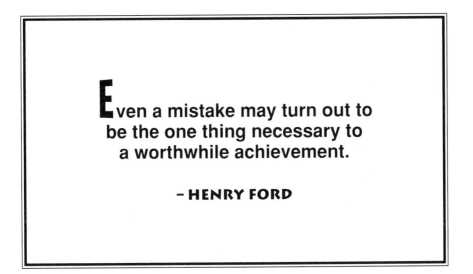

Even a mistake may turn out to
be the one thing necessary to
a worthwhile achievement.

– HENRY FORD

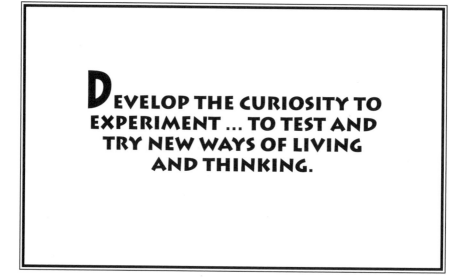

DEVELOP THE CURIOSITY TO EXPERIMENT ... TO TEST AND TRY NEW WAYS OF LIVING AND THINKING.

Develop success from failures.
Discouragement and failure are two of
the surest stepping stones to success. No
other element can do so much for a man if
he is willing to study them and make
capital out of them.

– DALE CARNEGIE

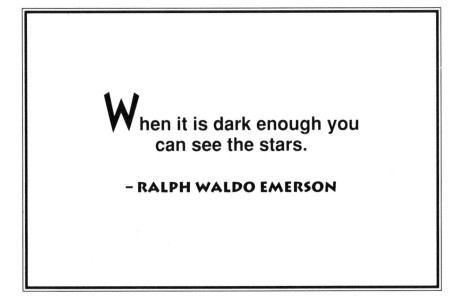

When it is dark enough you can see the stars.

– RALPH WALDO EMERSON

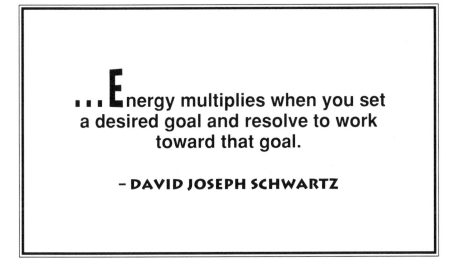

...**E**nergy multiplies when you set
a desired goal and resolve to work
toward that goal.

– DAVID JOSEPH SCHWARTZ

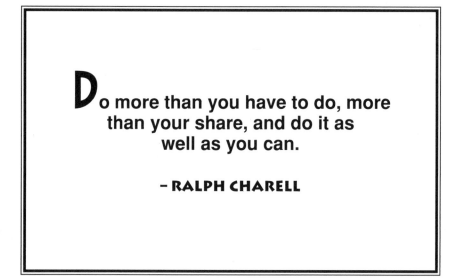

Do more than you have to do, more than your share, and do it as well as you can.

– RALPH CHARELL

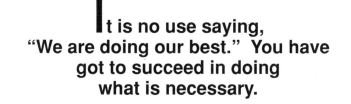

It is no use saying,
"We are doing our best." You have
got to succeed in doing
what is necessary.

– WINSTON CHURCHILL

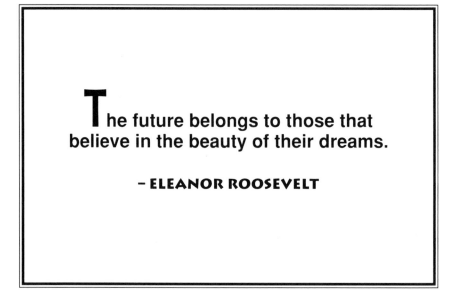

The future belongs to those that believe in the beauty of their dreams.

– ELEANOR ROOSEVELT

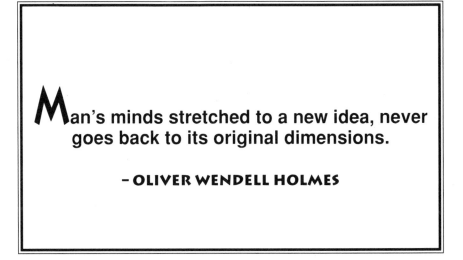

Man's minds stretched to a new idea, never goes back to its original dimensions.

– OLIVER WENDELL HOLMES

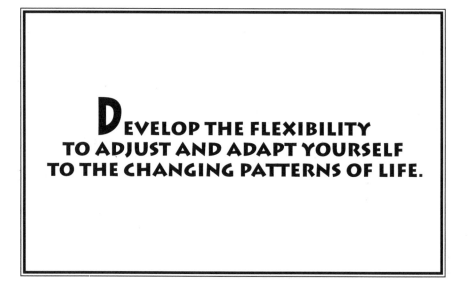

DEVELOP THE FLEXIBILITY
TO ADJUST AND ADAPT YOURSELF
TO THE CHANGING PATTERNS OF LIFE.

Hit the ball over the fence
and you can take your time
going around the bases.

– JOHN RAPER

First we will be best,
and then we will be first.

– GRANT TINKER

Once you say you're going to settle for second, that's what happens to you in life, I find.

— JOHN F. KENNEDY

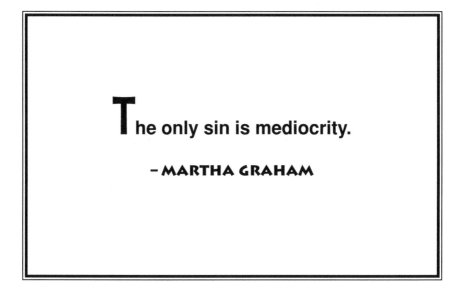

The only sin is mediocrity.

- MARTHA GRAHAM

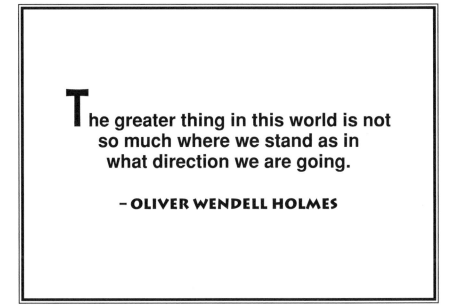

The greater thing in this world is not
so much where we stand as in
what direction we are going.

– OLIVER WENDELL HOLMES

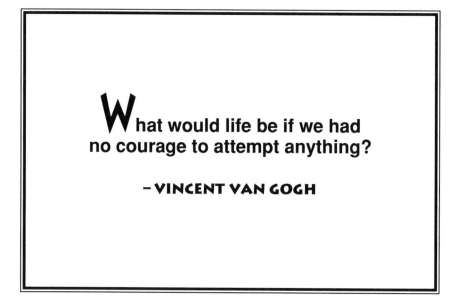

What would life be if we had
no courage to attempt anything?

– VINCENT VAN GOGH

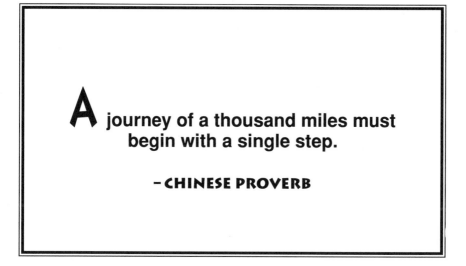

A journey of a thousand miles must begin with a single step.

– CHINESE PROVERB

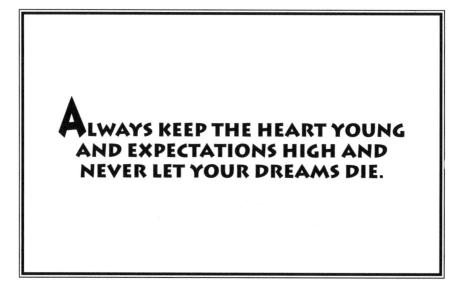

ALWAYS KEEP THE HEART YOUNG AND EXPECTATIONS HIGH AND NEVER LET YOUR DREAMS DIE.

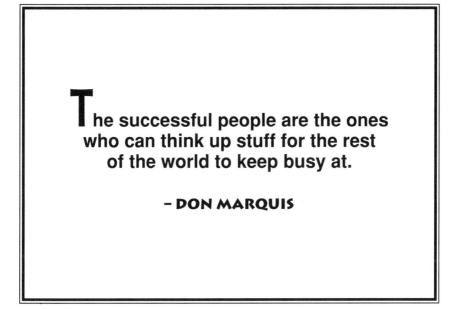

The successful people are the ones who can think up stuff for the rest of the world to keep busy at.

– DON MARQUIS

73

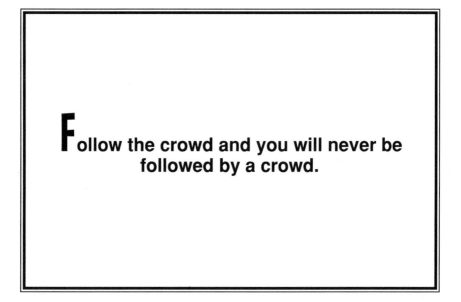

Follow the crowd and you will never be
followed by a crowd.

A person who walks in another's track leaves no footprints.

75

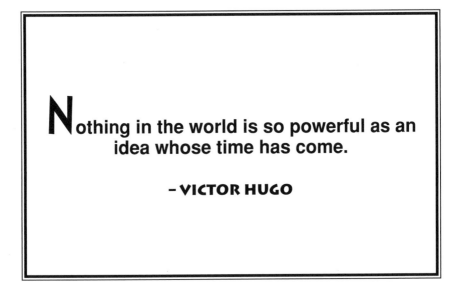

Nothing in the world is so powerful as an idea whose time has come.

– VICTOR HUGO

Don't wait for your ship to come in;
swim out to it.

Every thing comes to him
who hustles while he waits.

– THOMAS EDISON

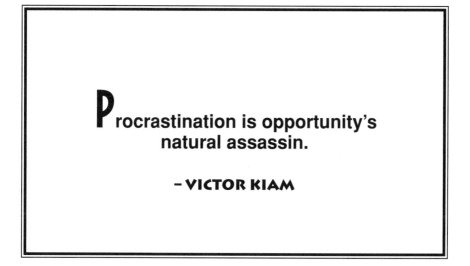

Procrastination is opportunity's
natural assassin.

– VICTOR KIAM

BE WILLING TO OPEN NEW DOORS
TO NEW EXPERIENCES AND TO STEP
BOLDLY FORTH TO EXPLORE
STRANGE NEW HORIZONS.

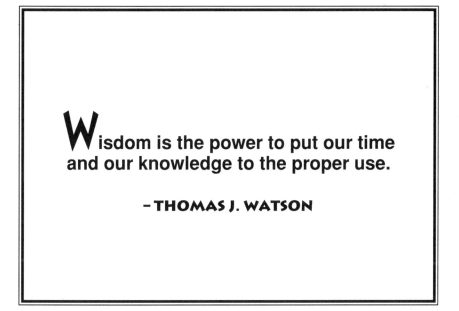

Wisdom is the power to put our time and our knowledge to the proper use.

– THOMAS J. WATSON

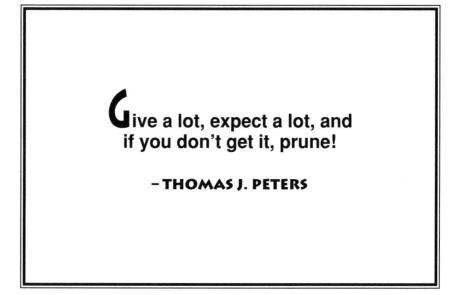

Give a lot, expect a lot, and
if you don't get it, prune!

– THOMAS J. PETERS

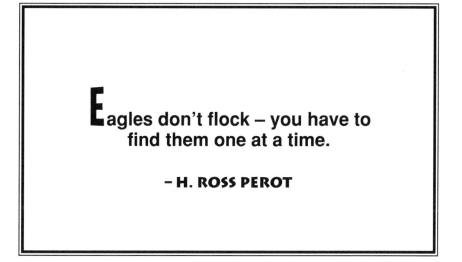

Eagles don't flock – you have to
find them one at a time.

– H. ROSS PEROT

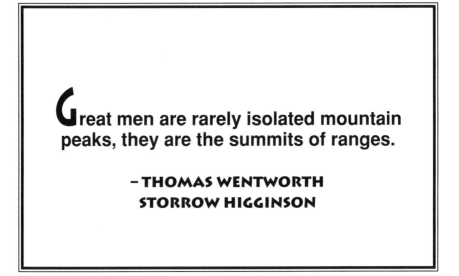

Great men are rarely isolated mountain peaks, they are the summits of ranges.

– THOMAS WENTWORTH STORROW HIGGINSON

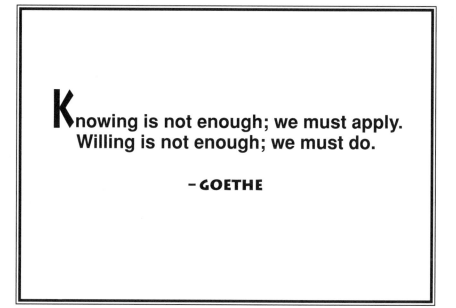

Knowing is not enough; we must apply.
Willing is not enough; we must do.

– GOETHE

Showing up is 80 percent of life.

– WOODY ALLEN

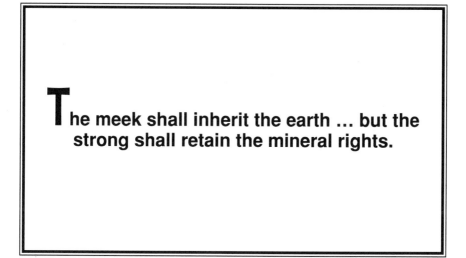

The meek shall inherit the earth ... but the strong shall retain the mineral rights.

ACCEPT THE CHALLENGE OF
MOUNTAIN-TOP TASKS AND GLORY
IN A JOB WELL-DONE.

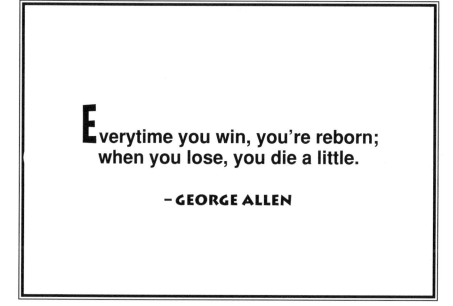

Everytime you win, you're reborn;
when you lose, you die a little.

– GEORGE ALLEN

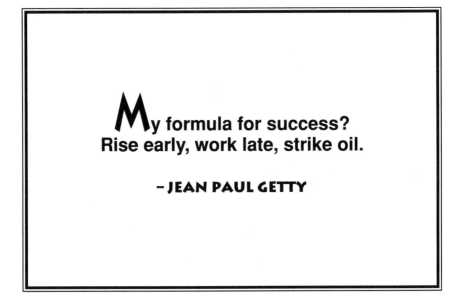

My formula for success?
Rise early, work late, strike oil.

– JEAN PAUL GETTY

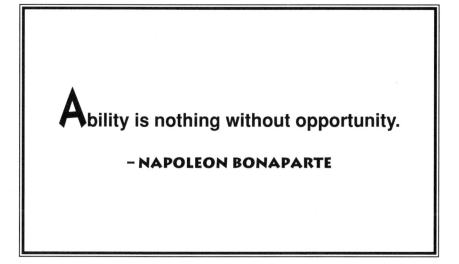

Ability is nothing without opportunity.

- NAPOLEON BONAPARTE

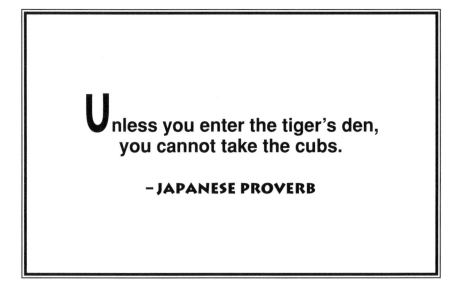

Unless you enter the tiger's den,
you cannot take the cubs.

– JAPANESE PROVERB

Don't be afraid to take a big step.
You can't cross a chasm in
two small jumps.

I like to work; it fascinates me.
I can sit and look at it for hours.

– JEROME K. JEROME

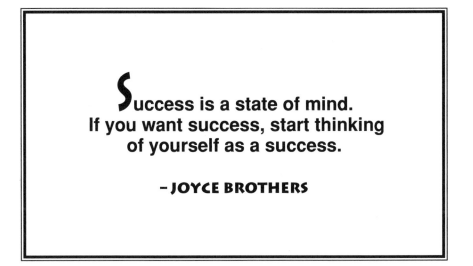

Success is a state of mind.
If you want success, start thinking
of yourself as a success.

– JOYCE BROTHERS

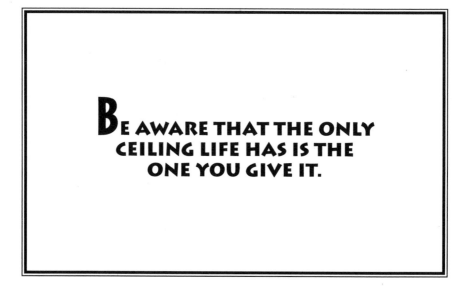

BE AWARE THAT THE ONLY
CEILING LIFE HAS IS THE
ONE YOU GIVE IT.

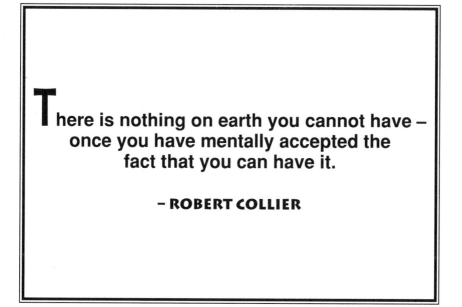

There is nothing on earth you cannot have –
once you have mentally accepted the
fact that you can have it.

– ROBERT COLLIER

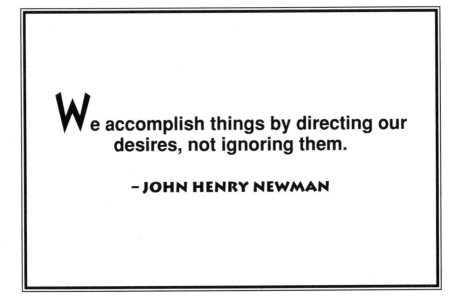

We accomplish things by directing our desires, not ignoring them.

– JOHN HENRY NEWMAN

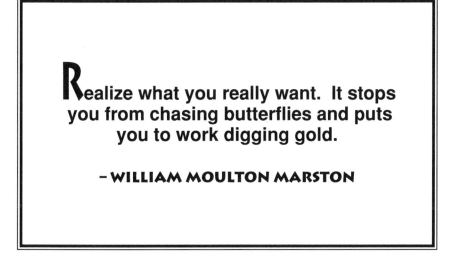

Realize what you really want. It stops
you from chasing butterflies and puts
you to work digging gold.

– WILLIAM MOULTON MARSTON

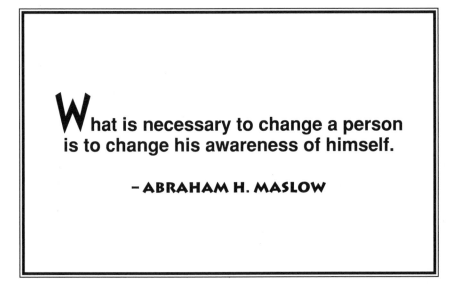

What is necessary to change a person
is to change his awareness of himself.

– ABRAHAM H. MASLOW

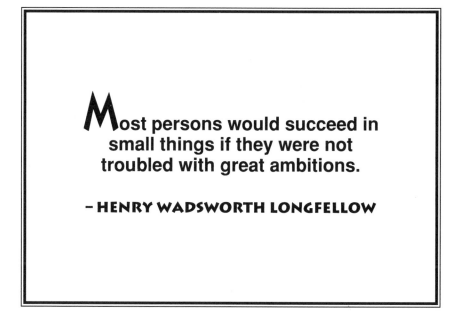

Most persons would succeed in small things if they were not troubled with great ambitions.

– HENRY WADSWORTH LONGFELLOW

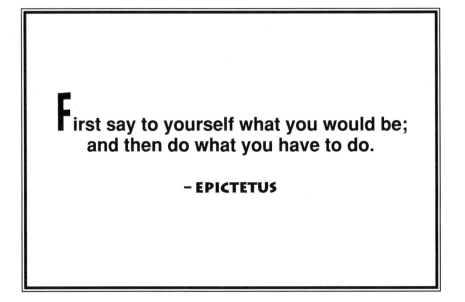

First say to yourself what you would be;
and then do what you have to do.

– **EPICTETUS**

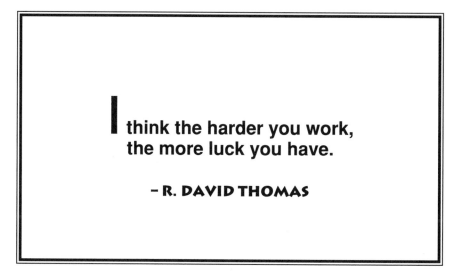

I think the harder you work,
the more luck you have.

– R. DAVID THOMAS

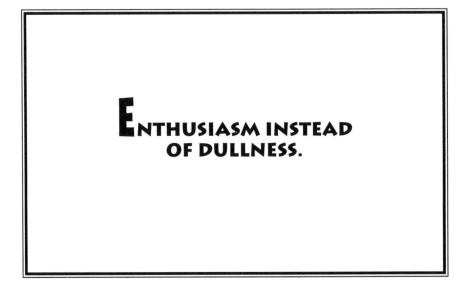

ENTHUSIASM INSTEAD
OF DULLNESS.

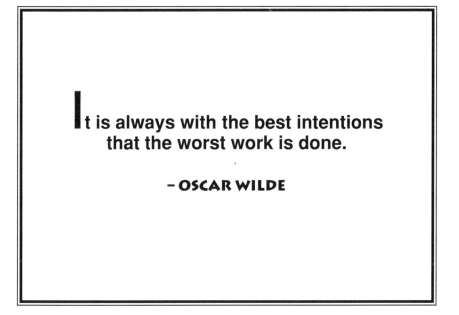

It is always with the best intentions
that the worst work is done.

– OSCAR WILDE

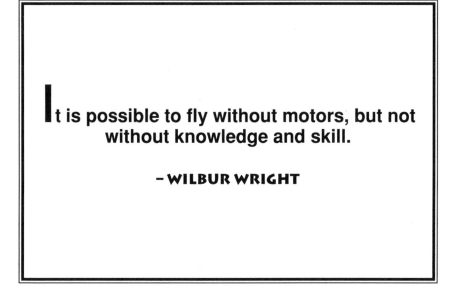

It is possible to fly without motors, but not without knowledge and skill.

– WILBUR WRIGHT

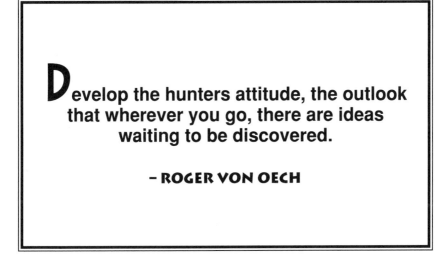

Develop the hunters attitude, the outlook
that wherever you go, there are ideas
waiting to be discovered.

– ROGER VON OECH

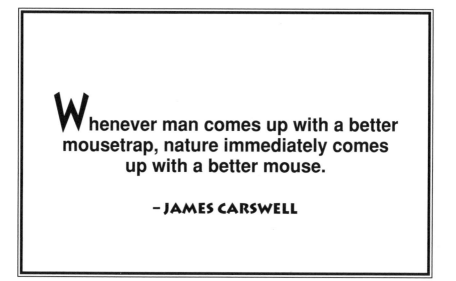

Whenever man comes up with a better
mousetrap, nature immediately comes
up with a better mouse.

– JAMES CARSWELL

Is life worth living? It is, if you take the risk of getting up in the morning and going through the day's work.

-WALTER PERSEGATI

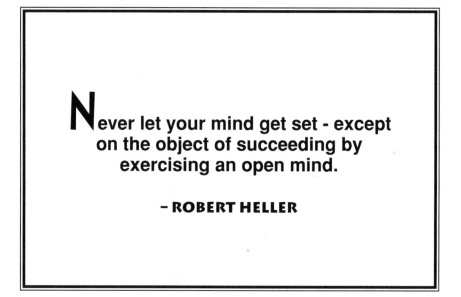

Never let your mind get set - except on the object of succeeding by exercising an open mind.

– ROBERT HELLER

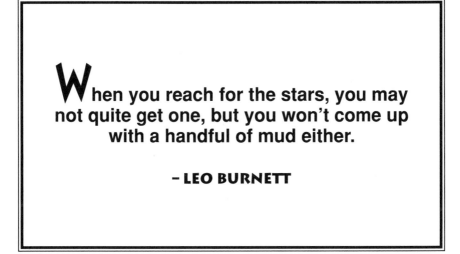

When you reach for the stars, you may not quite get one, but you won't come up with a handful of mud either.

– LEO BURNETT

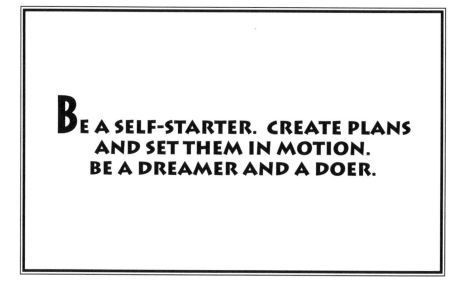

BE A SELF-STARTER. CREATE PLANS
AND SET THEM IN MOTION.
BE A DREAMER AND A DOER.

Some people dream of worthy accomplishments, while others stay awake and do them.

I can always be distracted by love, but eventually I get horny for my creativity.

– GILDA RADNER

A hunch is creativity trying to tell you something.

– FRANK CAPRA

One doesn't discover new lands without
consenting to lose sight of the shore
for a very long time.

– ANDRE GILDE

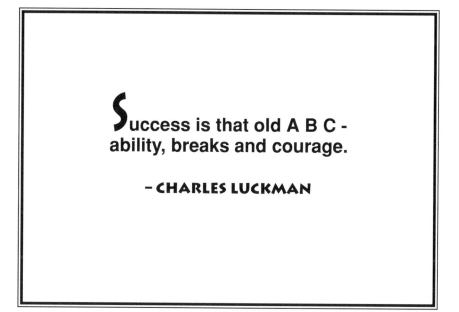

Success is that old A B C -
ability, breaks and courage.

– CHARLES LUCKMAN

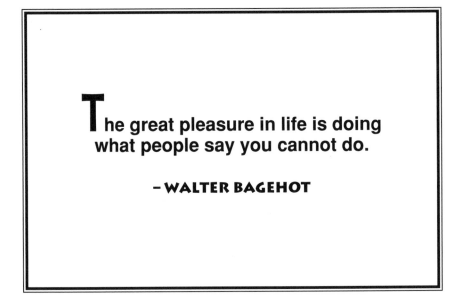

T he great pleasure in life is doing
what people say you cannot do.

– WALTER BAGEHOT

The road to success is dotted with many tempting parking spaces.

HAVE FAITH IN PEOPLE.
BELIEVE IN THEM, TRUST THEM
AND YOU WILL DRAW OUT THE
BEST IN THEM. THEY WILL RISE HIGH
TO YOUR EXPECTATIONS.

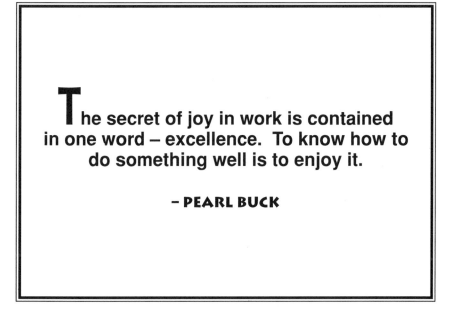

The secret of joy in work is contained in one word — excellence. To know how to do something well is to enjoy it.

– PEARL BUCK

Behind every successful man is a woman who keeps reminding him that she knows men who would have done even better.

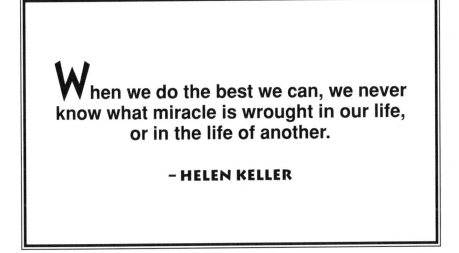

When we do the best we can, we never know what miracle is wrought in our life, or in the life of another.

– HELEN KELLER

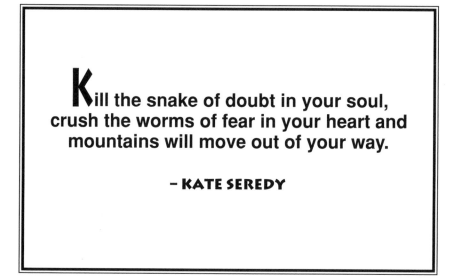

Kill the snake of doubt in your soul,
crush the worms of fear in your heart and
mountains will move out of your way.

– KATE SEREDY

No matter what the level of ability, you have more potential than you can ever develop in a lifetime.

– JAMES T. M^CCAY

There are powers inside of you which, if you could discover and use, would make of you everything you ever dreamed or imagined you could become.

– ORISON SWETT MARDEN

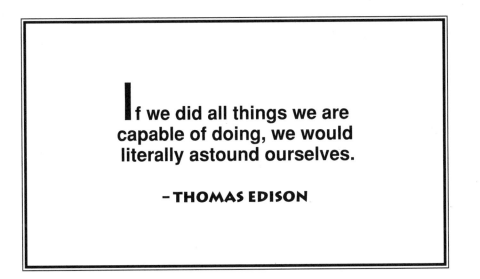

If we did all things we are
capable of doing, we would
literally astound ourselves.

- THOMAS EDISON

127

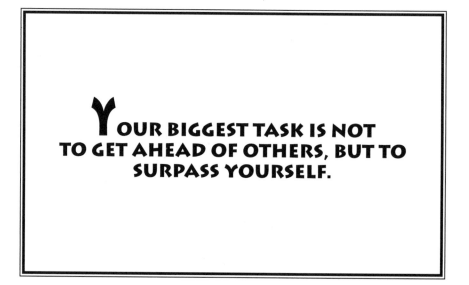

YOUR BIGGEST TASK IS NOT TO GET AHEAD OF OTHERS, BUT TO SURPASS YOURSELF.

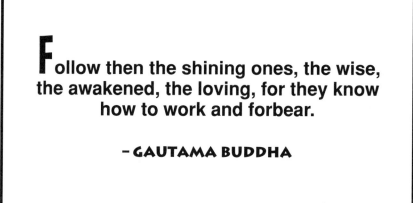

Follow then the shining ones, the wise, the awakened, the loving, for they know how to work and forbear.

– GAUTAMA BUDDHA

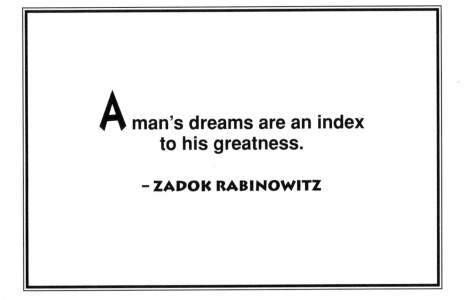

A man's dreams are an index to his greatness.

– ZADOK RABINOWITZ

The only way to discover the limits of the possible is to go beyond them into the impossible.

– ARTHUR C. CLARKE

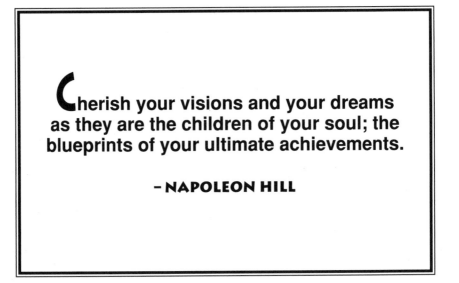

Cherish your visions and your dreams
as they are the children of your soul; the
blueprints of your ultimate achievements.

– NAPOLEON HILL

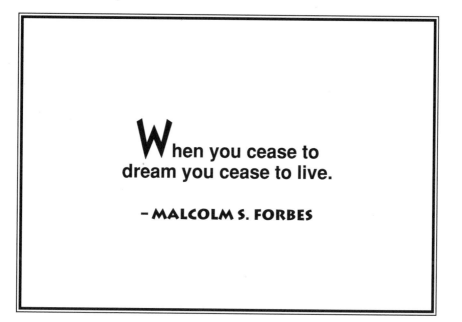

When you cease to
dream you cease to live.

— MALCOLM S. FORBES

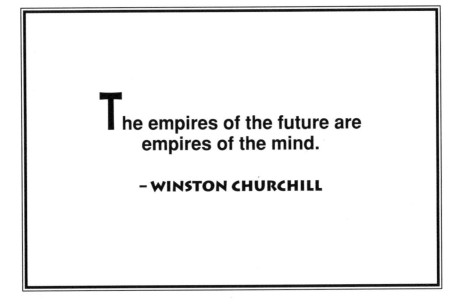

The empires of the future are
empires of the mind.

– WINSTON CHURCHILL

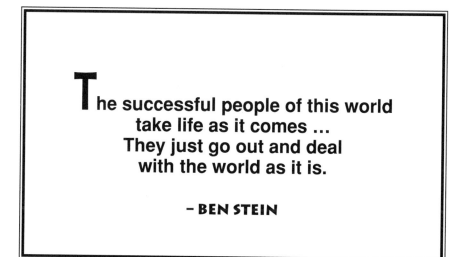

The successful people of this world
take life as it comes ...
They just go out and deal
with the world as it is.

– BEN STEIN

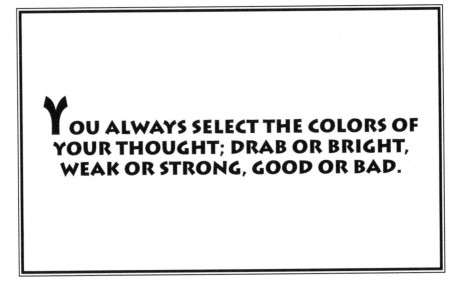

YOU ALWAYS SELECT THE COLORS OF YOUR THOUGHT; DRAB OR BRIGHT, WEAK OR STRONG, GOOD OR BAD.

Always do your best.
What you plant now, you
will harvest later.

– OG MANDINO

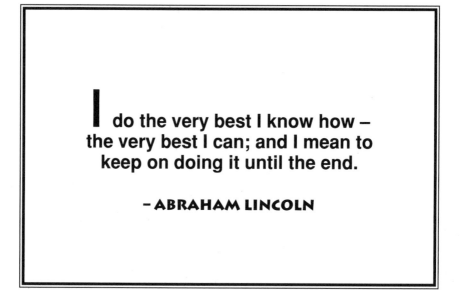

I do the very best I know how —
the very best I can; and I mean to
keep on doing it until the end.

– ABRAHAM LINCOLN

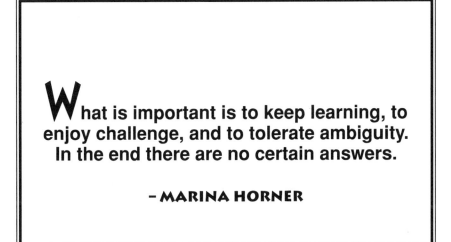

What is important is to keep learning, to enjoy challenge, and to tolerate ambiguity. In the end there are no certain answers.

– MARINA HORNER

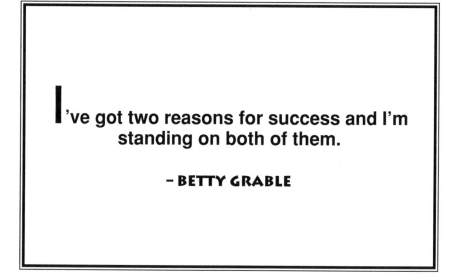

I've got two reasons for success and I'm standing on both of them.

– BETTY GRABLE

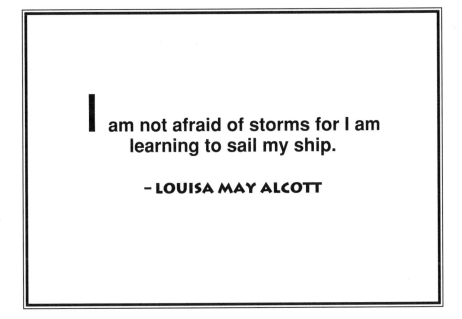

I am not afraid of storms for I am learning to sail my ship.

– LOUISA MAY ALCOTT

The men who try to do something and fail are infinitely better than those who try to do nothing and succeed.

– LLOYD JONES

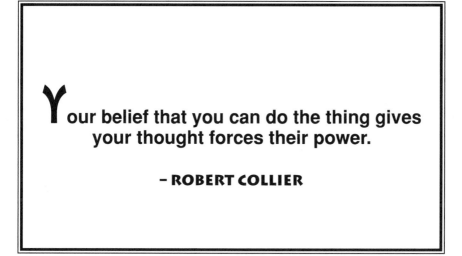

Your belief that you can do the thing gives your thought forces their power.

– ROBERT COLLIER

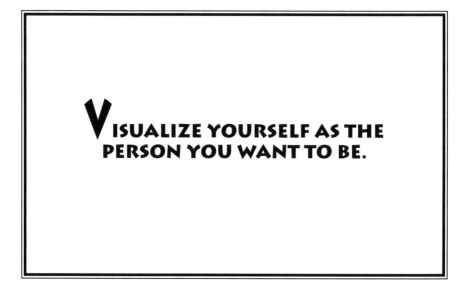

VISUALIZE YOURSELF AS THE PERSON YOU WANT TO BE.

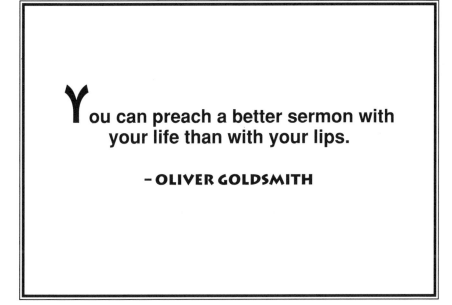

You can preach a better sermon with your life than with your lips.

- OLIVER GOLDSMITH

You must be single minded. Drive for the one thing on which you have decided.

- GEORGE S. PATTON

Each moment of your life is a brush
stroke in the painting of
your growing career.

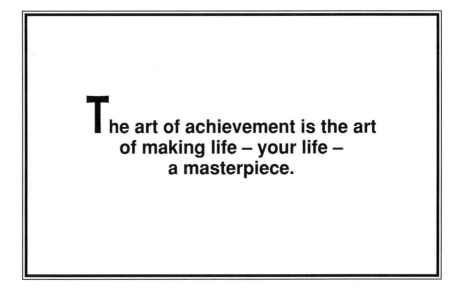

The art of achievement is the art of making life – your life – a masterpiece.

There are no secrets to success.
Success is doing the things
you know you should do.

Don't confuse activity
with accomplishments.

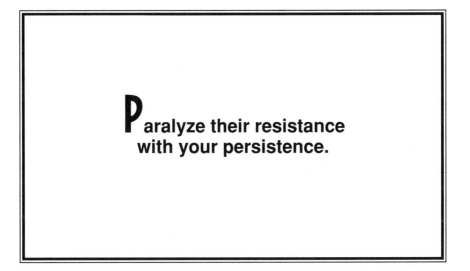

Paralyze their resistance
with your persistence.

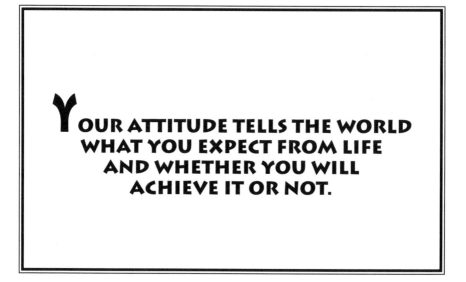

YOUR ATTITUDE TELLS THE WORLD
WHAT YOU EXPECT FROM LIFE
AND WHETHER YOU WILL
ACHIEVE IT OR NOT.

Take the initiative and work hard.
Ask questions, look for opportunity
but don't wait for success
to come to you.

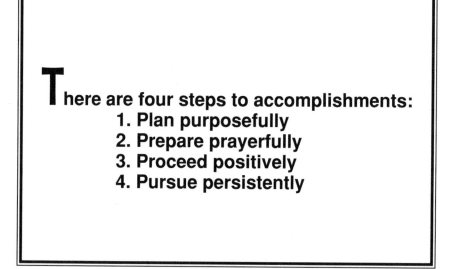

There are four steps to accomplishments:
1. Plan purposefully
2. Prepare prayerfully
3. Proceed positively
4. Pursue persistently

Your life can't go according to plan if you have no plan.

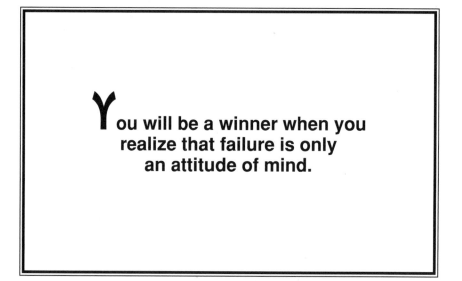

You will be a winner when you
realize that failure is only
an attitude of mind.

If you want a place in the sun,
you will have to
expect some blisters.

Don't measure yourself by what you have accomplished, but what you should have accomplished with your ability.

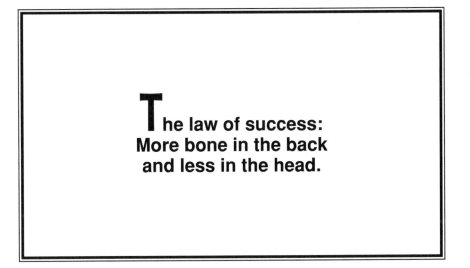

The law of success:
More bone in the back
and less in the head.

Your rewards in life are always in
direct proportion to
your contribution.

A gem cannot be polished without friction, nor man perfected without trials.

Fear is created not by the world around us, but in the mind, by what we think is going to happen.

If better is possible,
good is not enough.

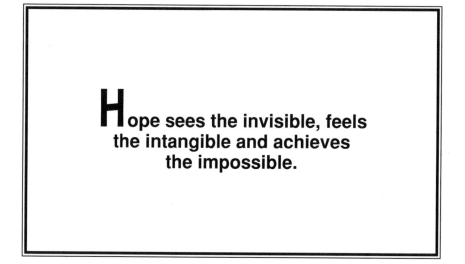

Hope sees the invisible, feels
the intangible and achieves
the impossible.

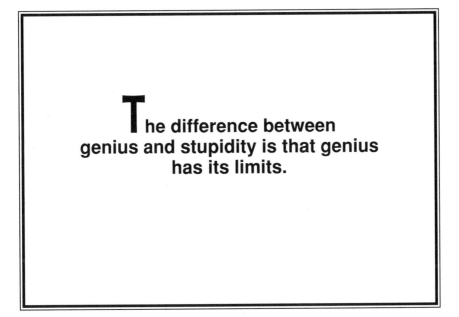

The difference between genius and stupidity is that genius has its limits.

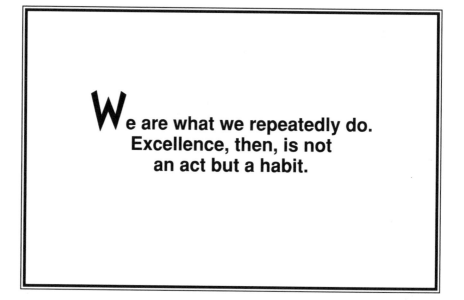

We are what we repeatedly do.
Excellence, then, is not
an act but a habit.

Every job is a self-portrait
of the person who did it.
Autograph your work
with excellence.

Other Titles By Great Quotations

201 Best Things Ever Said
The ABC's of Parenting
As a Cat Thinketh
The Best of Friends
The Birthday Astrologer
Chicken Soup & Other Yiddish Say
Cornerstones of Success
Don't Deliberate ... Litigate!
Fantastic Father, Dependable Dad
Global Wisdom
Golden Years, Golden Words
Grandma, I Love You
Growing up in Toyland
Happiness is Found Along The Way
Hollywords
Hooked on Golf
In Celebration of Women
Inspirations Compelling Food for Thought
I'm Not Over the Hill
Let's Talk Decorating
Life's Lessons
Life's Simple Pleasures
A Light Heart Lives Long
Money for Nothing, Tips for Free

Mother, I Love You
Motivating Quotes for Motivated People
Mrs. Aesop's Fables
Mrs. Murphy's Laws
Mrs. Webster's Dictionary
My Daughter, My Special Friend
Other Species
Parenting 101
Reflections
Romantic Rhapsody
The Secret Language of Men
The Secret Language of Women
Some Things Never Change
The Sports Page
Sports Widow
Stress or Sanity
Teacher is Better than Two Books
Teenage of Insanity
Thanks from the Heart
Things You'll Learn if You Live Long Enough
Wedding Wonders
Working Women's World
Interior Design for Idiots
Dear Mr. President

GREAT QUOTATIONS PUBLISHING COMPANY
1967 Quincy Court
Glendale Heights, IL 60139 - 2045
Phone (630) 582-2800
Fax (630) 582- 2813